A Heart's Dissection

Serenity Tia

BookLeaf Publishing

India | USA | UK

Made with ❤ on the BookLeaf Publishing Platform
www.bookleafpub.in
www.bookleafpub.com

Dedication

This book is dedicated to my three loves, Ramiah,
Mariyah and River.
Also, to those who've been showing up for me, cheering
for me and loving me out loud
Thank you!

Preface

Why does a heart love? What makes a heart break? So many of us have trouble understanding why we love the way that we do, even if the love is never reciprocated. Why does a heart choose who it loves?

What makes a heart so cold? A Heart's Dissection is a book filled with inspiring poems about self-love, overcoming betrayal, heartbreaks and disloyalty. On each page I have opened up and shared a piece of my heart during each phase

of love, and because the feelings and thoughts surrounding the Word love are so broad, some pages may seem dark while others are light, uplifting and motivating. I invite you; my reader, to experience love through my eyes. you don't have to be a poet to understand and connect with my words as I'm no fancy poet I just write from the heart.

Acknowledgements

I would like to express my deepest gratitude to my supporters; all those who have partaken in my writing journey.

I would also like to extend my sincere thanks to every reader.

A Heart For Sale

Excuse me? How much would you pay for my heart?

"I'm sorry, but your heart is no token". "It has been used abused weakened and broken".
But you can fix it right?

"Fix it?" "You must be joking!" "This heart is stained with pain and taken for granted, and the label says preserve in 100 percent realness yet it's wrapped in plastic". "Besides, you're looking for full price for a half empty heart, you're wasting your time and your breath". "It's supposed to be filled with love but there's hardly any left; plus, it's toxic so good luck trying to give it away to anyone".

Why?"

"Because They'll just run, and to be honest", "It's not worth the work to make it new". "There's not much I'm willing to do".

But what makes you so sure, that my heart won't be worth more, to someone else than what it was?

"Because nobody wants a heart that the owner doesn't even love". "But like I said before, good luck and no thank you".
"You should try next door".

Excuse me? Are you looking for a heart? and before you answer, I don't want to sell it; I just want to replace it. Matter of Fact, here take it! Giving it away has been tough, I've giving all the love I can give but it's never enough.
It's too fragile, it's been refused, it's confused, it has never been flaunted; It attaches itself to people who don't even want it. I don't know maybe you could use the unwanted parts, maybe take it for disassembly, it doesn't fit me. Yes, it's big but
it's empty.

"So, let me get this straight, "You're still giving your heart away although it has been used and abused from the very beginning?" and all you want in return is the same love that you've been giving?" "See, no one has the same kind of heart
as you". "The love you give is rare". "It doesn't need changing just a little self-care". "It may have been used abused and broken, but the heart I see inside you is a God's given token". "You may have not taken care of it and others in the past may have treated it wrong, but it's

still full of love and it's still beating strong". "Yes, your heart may have gotten broken but it's fixable with the right person to patch it". It's not toxic, they only ran because they couldn't match it". "They saw all the love left they just chose to look past it". "They didn't want it to get away they weren't built to go after it". "If you're looking for a refund, I can't give you back the love you already gave, but I'm willing to exchange my heart as collateral while I mend those broken pieces; fill it up with my love and give it back to you". "But only you can make your heart worth more than it ever was". Nobody wants a heart that the owner doesn't even love".

We Were Just Fine

Waking up to your good morning text
Looking forward to dates that you would plan
Walks just to talk, my hand in your hand
Soft kisses feeling like magic, giving chills as you place
your jacket
across my shoulders
You're putting your hands around my waste I'm blushing
I'm wiping the lip gloss from your face you're crushing
you're gazing into my eyes and I'm looking away
Trying not to act phased by your seductive ways
 but got damn your handsome
 Then, I heard you speak Spanish and oh man
I know sex wasn't initially part of the plan
but you had me at Hola'
Days turned into months and although we weren't
rushing
or maybe just a little bit
But the words I love you snuck into our relationship
and we went to bed pretty happy
But we must've woken up on the wrong side of the bed
because
suddenly things got ugly
The nightmares started
The pointing fingers

The constant bashing
The outlashing
We were crashing
How did we end up here? Because we were just fine
Now, the arguing the crying
because you were always lying

I was not the only one

The constant blame left me feeling shamed
You were blurting out truths that left a sting
and, I couldn't say a thing
because,

You were not the only one

Displacement
fears of abandonment leaving our hearts racing
The back and forth the constant chasing
we have manifested our separation
But we were just fine
Had I known that we were running out of time
I'd pour one more glass of wine
and kissed your lips after every sip
but we just called it quits
and I must admit,
that I thought you'll come after me but instead
You just let me go and left me in my head
why you moved quickly on to the next
Got me thinking should I go back to my ex?

Refraining from sending you that wyd text
I don't want to be alone. Why are you ok without me?
Reminiscing of you dancing and me laughing
and you laughing at my jokes
would somehow give us hope
that we'd make it
but we faded
How did we end up here?

The Mattress of Regret

Today I decided to throw out my mattress
It was badly stained of regret
Insecurities, unwanted energies
A fountain of tears pouring heavily into my glass of
Moscato
That turned into another glass
and then bottle after bottle
False promises and eh, I'll call him tomorrow
although I never do
avoiding ties, to keep from absorbing lies
and an easy Fuck You
Sike come back I care
Nah, it's not true?
Probably not but deep down I want to
The words I love you had no meaning just letters from
the alphabet
Ok, my timer is set, this is just for fun
When it goes off, you are to exit
we're done!
But I allowed this one to stay just a little too long
my alarm clock had a morning notification tittle Regret
Damn he didn't call yet
Do I actually care? Maybe so

But to my mattress I was nothing more than a hoe
so yes, it had to go

Just Show Up

No, I don't need anything from the store
You don't need to impress me with gifts of galore
And although I'm a sucker for flowers that's not what
this is about
Cause' if the presents are the reason you're not currently
in my presence
Then i can do without
Being the man you are, I know you pride yourself on not
showing up empty handed
but i prefer them to be free
Cause' your warm embrace is actually enough for me
You do enough for me,
Baby you are enough for me, come talk to me
Tell me, how was your day?
we don't have to talk about it if you don't want
We can play your video games
While you wait for dinner and your bath water's hot
You could probably tell that I missed you a lot
Come laugh with me
I'm sure your heart could use some company
My mind could use a friend
My soul could use a mate
Let me in
Allow me to find the pieces of you, you lost while you

were broken

I want to see you whole

And I'm down to have some fun except i don't want to play around with your feelings

guide me to your soul

Teach me your love language and I'll speak it fluently

Help me to understand your heart, introduce the you to me

You don't understand what you do to me

The way you walk with your head up high even when things go bad

How you still find the strength to console me when I'm feeling sad

The way that you Silence your haters and Nay Sayers

The way you take my hand in prayer, Good God!

You get it done I have never saw you run

 I want you to know that you are not alone

Allow me to get you warmed up and set the emotional tone

You get these little pom poms clapping

I am your cheer captain tonight

Put your worries to the side it's alright, I know what you like

Lay down and let me distract you, you can even roll one

It's the power of your tongue

Your positivity, I love how you show that you're into me

Your energy has gotten in to me and I caught a contact

now, I'm so high, I probably could fly and all of that
Now, I'm not saying that I don't love to be spoiled
and I won't pretend that that isn't me
But you deserve someone who's going to reciprocate
your energy,
I can tell that you're really feeling me
And I'm feeling you too
but you're always making it about me so what about
you?
So, whatever you're doing just get here

A Heart's Dissection

Why do you fear love when it comes to you?
Why do you run?
Have you not had your heart protected?
I'm talking more than just your pericardium
Have you had trouble in the past, knowing the difference
from the real thing and a TAH?
Who's been tricking ya?
Was it one person in particular?
Because you've been opening up and shutting, opening
up and shutting
like the Atrioventricular
Have you always been your own epicardium?
Is that why no one's made you feel safe?
Has no one acted as the thing to your heart that controls
the rhythm and pace?
(You know your electrical conduct system)
Has no one taken the time, to go through your mind, to
connect with your heart?
(You know acting as the Vagus nerve)
Or did you let them skip that part?
Why do you fear life?
Is it because you're afraid that you won't find the thing
that makes you feel like living?
Do you breathe at the beginning, of each awakening

moment?
Do you hold your breath, decreasing your heartbeat?
waiting for the one who will make your heart weak, and
that is why you're killing yourself
Anything that makes the heart weak was never good for
your health
C.A.D
The next person who "touches" your heart, ask them
what it feels like
Was it intentional? are they really into you?
Are you allowing the right people to enter you?
When your heart beats faster, is it from the sensual or
sexual?
Be careful, of what lays next to you
There are many ways to open a heart
and some prefer the scalpel

A Solo Coffee date

*Closing old doors, replacing old locks and throwing
away old keys
That once welcomed unhealthy attachments to people
who came and gone as they pleased
No more bonding over traumas
I would rather have my coffee sitting across from
someone serious about our future
Someone who gives back a little more than excuses
The window of opportunity I once left cracked open for
just in case purposes
blew nothing in but constant disappointment so I shut it
My new doors don't come with peep holes
My new shoes got new soles, and I will walk away!
My maybes were foreign, and sometimes ignoring,
would send mixed messages
so, I've learned to be precise
you know like thanks for the invite, but I'm not going
I would rather have my coffee alone
then to sit at a table with those who find me boring
Not truly invested, or connected
Just lonely*

I Heard Death Call

The sound sent chills
Crows landed at my doorstep; they circled the air above
me
A black feather fell at my feet
Darkness climbed in bed with me, dreams of me falling
Fear traveled through me faster than the speed of light
Anxiety, spread through my body, like a virus
Whenever I stepped outside of my home I panicked
experiencing manic
negativity planted, its nest inside of my head,
Housing an infestation of negative thoughts
I couldn't silence them
Is today the day?
Something said kneel and pray
I know the devil is a liar!
God isn't finished with me yet!
you can't have me, or my family
you can take my job; I'll get another one
You can take my car; I'll get another one
But you can Not have me, I shall live and not die
I Looked death in the eye
Today will not be the day!
God isn't finished with me yet
Suddenly, the sounds I heard

were just sounds of birds
The skies were clear
Fear, became peace
I was able to breathe and live free once again

What Love Is

*You have no clue what love is, and I can't be the one to
teach you
If you don't love yourself then I can't be the one to please
you
still, I go the extra mile just to see you smile
and somehow, I still can't reach you
I'm not wasting time trying to preach to you
Cause' you got major pride
Scared to face yourself so you're quick to run and hide
Your traumas have been a burden
Your burdens have weighed too much
Pain has made you numb to life, so you don't feel my
touch
You can't feel that I care
You don't see that I'm there; I've been invisible
your past is keeping you miserable
I can't ask what's gotten in to you
You never seemed to change
I hate that you're in pain, but I can't be the one to blame
At times our connection is lit
Then you come putting out the flame
you're scared to trust; all we do if fuss
I won't apologize for the both of us
so, you would rather us give up*

You don't know what love is
Cold as Ice so its hurt people hurt people
You say this isn't the real you
But you don't know what love is
and I can't be the one to heal you

Game Of Blame (a Game of Thrones inspired piece)

What am I worth?
When it seems, I was cursed at birth
Growing inside of my mother's wound, didn't heal her
wounds
A seed grown from the trauma; of my father she was
burying
Sick from the burdens she was carrying I too am Tyrion
Because,
Because,
She chose me, giving up her dreams
When I was born it seems, I took her life away

Its's my fault, for knowing I was a single mother with
two kids
and still decided to add one
But why would I lay down, looking up at the moon and
stars and then give up my son?
some say that I be dragging, I shouldn't be bragging
Call me Daenerys, cause' where would a mother be
without her three dragons
My kids are fire

If I say mothering isn't hard, then I may be a liar
Struck by lightning, rained upon, the earth cracked
beneath my feet
but I withstood the storm, I too am storm born

My name has been drug through the streets
Stripped of morals, dignity, beliefs; like I am the only one
who makes mistakes
Why should God punish me? Say that I am the face of
shame
a walk of atonement to curse me
I too am Cersei
Stubborn, I will stand my ground and blow this place
down
They must not know who they're dealing with. I will
protect my crown
at all costs

It's my own fault
My own Tribe stood in line to stab me in the heart
Many so-called friends laughed as I fell apart
Knowing I went to hell and back for them
I clapped for them
I fought for them and had their backs, when they didn't
know what they were up against
I stood ten toes down! But they stood, as my big beating
heart bled

From my trials they fed, and then they fled
They left me to die, as if I wasn't coming back from the
dead
Like don't y'all know that I will hang up' my friendships
form alliances and turn enemies into allies
I will rise high from my lows
I too am John Snow
Realized I was Greater
They all became traitors
Found out I was even sleeping with a hater

Tired of having to put on many faces just to be, whom I
really want to be
Who am I?
A girl is, to blame for those who won't accept
accountability
Surprised at my abilities
Shocked that a girl, is one who would save the world
If only I had known my purpose from the start
I too am Arya Stark
It's not my fault, It's not my fault. I told myself I'm not
the one doing it
Love is the death of duty, and I have a duty to myself
To do what's best for me over anything else
Because, when it's all said and done
 they'll choose themselves
and I will still be the one to blame

Bed Time Stories

I was just a little kid
Watching the monsters who pried under my bed
They knew me
They'd wait until bedtime to read me stories
one in particular,
The Three Little pigs; Little pig little pig let me in
And I would say
Not by the hair of my chinny, chin, chin
But the Wolf would enter on its own
And I had no other home to run too
All of my favorite childhood stories became nightmares
After the stories the real stories were just beginning
I was always envious of other kids when they would
speak of fairytales
Because the ones told to me had no happy endings

A Fling called Poetry

Poetry, you are my side boo.
We click in bed, but I can't have you stick around
For a second you have my juices flowing
When It's done, I come, and then kick you to the side
for a little while

I know you want to be more than just a fling
You want to get close to me, but I'm distracted by other
things
See, my main boo is life. I'm afraid to tell life
That I've been creeping at night, with you
That I've had an affair, because you were there
When I needed someone to talk to
To be vulnerable

You don't judge, There's no grudge
We relate a little more
But there's a revolving door
Because life has my time, but you stay on my mind

You, fill a void for me, but
Life has my loyalty
Life gets in my head
Life has my kids

So, I can't just walk away

When life and I are fighting and there's no hiding
poetry, you are my escape
You bring me peace,
you put my mind at ease
I want to be with you,
but life has a hold on me
oh, I wish the 3 of us be poly

Poetry you are the gift that isn't compensated
you are available whenever I call
But I can't give you my all
Because life just needs me more

Day 1

Day one
It is repetitive like a single beat of a drum
it comes and goes like the sound of thunder, while I out
wait the storm
It is the relapse of rehab
The equivalence of Deja vu; I could have sworn I've been
here before
It is the rewind of time and the reset; but it never stops
It is persistent
it is one step in the right direction and one step
backwards
but it doesn't quit
It is the start of something new
The key to perfection
proof of your existence
proof that you're human
proof that you're trying
Right?
I'm just trying to convince myself that it's Alright
because
After many days of crying, healing and praying
I went back to you
I should have known that the cycle would never end
and we'd be doing this once again

and here I am
needing to heal all over again
Back at day 1, so let's began
Again

I've Changed

Something about me has changed
My smile seems the same
But the light in my eyes has dimmed a bit
I don't laugh as much
I have been out of touch with the old me
Not feeling as cheery, as i used to
But somewhere inside
There's the biggest smile I ever smiled
I Badly want to free it
They all look at me and see this glow
but I really don't really see it
I can hear the whispering
Oh Man she's transitioning
But I miss the old me

The Beast I've Once Feared

I stood face to face with my fears
Tiptoed through the dark, so those who saw me as light
would not witness me dropping the load of the burdens
that I could barely hold
But I am not ashamed
Not to preach, but I've been pulling strings for people
who wouldn't bend down to tie my shoes
If I could no longer reach, Because
They would rather see me trip and fall; surrounded by
walls of the holes I had to dig myself from
I couldn't let them see me hang my head, so I had to cut
ties loose
I reached out my hand and got bitten by snakes
but I am a mongoose; you would not see me lose
I have turned words into blades, and I've allowed them to
sink into my skin but again
I am not ashamed, because
overtime scars will fade, and I am proud of the warrior
life has made
And now
I am a walking bullet proof vest
Negativity taking shots at me, but I am aiming for the
best
I am a pluviophile

*I burry my face in the rain and let it pour but still I smile,
because*
Not all storms come to interrupt your life
*Sometimes it's just what we need because, if you weren't
looking forward to the rain*
Why would you even plant the seed?
*Let me say again that not all storms come to interrupt
your life*
*Instead, it falls to restore all of the faith lost when you
couldn't see growth*
*How come we only look forward to sunshine to give us
hope, during our dullest seasons?*
*Understand that everything that is happening is for a
reason*
*I've lost friends for a reason, my job for a reason,
relationships for a reason*
caught a flat but had a spare
looked around nobody was there
I remember when BGE turned off my air
But dammit I'm still breathing
My whole existence is for a reason
*My daughter's existence gave me something to believe in
myself*
*I drop my head to hearing a hundred of mommy, can
you?*
But if I can't then who else?
My plate has been empty, yet I say no to their offer

I don't get my hopes high, so I won't be disappointed
With nothing, I pay my ties and keep hope in most high
so, I am covered by thee Annointed
I am resilient, made in his image I rise like the sun
Y'all better set your alarm clocks because
I am not the one to be sleeping on. I was born great
I had a beautiful date with fate, and fell in love with the
blood, that flows through my veins
I am taking lessons from my losses but focused on my
gains
Shout out to the part of me who went ghost when I
needed her most
and now, as I look into the mirror, I am happy to see her
reappear
There is no sight more beautiful than standing face to
face
Looking at the beast that I use to fear

The ones who left

To the people who left when I was at my lowest
Wasn't focused
Battling depression
Constant rejection
When all I wanted was someone to give me a chance
To all those who laughed, at my dreams
who shot down my visions
Couldn't see the gift that I have been given
when I was stuck in rough seasons
fighting demons
when I was
To week to speak
Had no food to eat
To those who dug my grave, when I didn't know if I
wanted to live
The ones who left my side because I had nothing left to
give
When I struggled to stay sane for my kids
You left
My tears caused you stress
And even as I went through my worse days
All I asked, was that you'd be patient with me
Pray for me
believe in my journey

Clap for me

Stay True

But you chose to go and that's on you

Don't Go Back

You're afraid,
and although you say you'll be ok
I can hear the fear in your thoughts
but you had to walk away
now, where do you go?
You walk into the dark of the unknown
Scared that you'll be snatched, by something much worse
The familiar is calling you back
The surrounding of your own shadows
make you feel like you'll end up alone
The past is calling you home
For a second you glance back
But you can't go back, there's nothing left there for you
now, what do you do?
Remember all the pain your old life gave
You must be brave
You keep moving forward
But at a very slow pace
giving them time to catch up to you
I can hear your heart race
I know you're in an uncomfortable place
But you can't go back
You're afraid
But you keep moving forward

Then suddenly, you're met with sunshine
and everything you've left behind
has shattered to pieces
But you survived
I'm glad
you didn't
go back

Self Developing

The other day I took a selfie
But I didn't use my iPhone
I couldn't add a filter
AI couldn't create lies
I was forced to be faced to face with the truth
I carefully examined what I was looking at
I noticed that
There's a little darkness where there should be light
You know "Negative"
Didn't quite seem my best but I am a work in progress
I've been loud when I should've been quiet
I hung with the wrong crowds
I stayed hidden with people who should have loved me
out loud
I forgot to Keep God first
I would thirst for everything except what was actually
fulfilling to me
I spoke negatively, about myself
ignored my health
I forgot about me
My inner algorithm has been connecting me with people
who matched the way
I looked at myself
EWW

The selfie lacked confidence

A bunch of pettiness

Very Immature

Not Very cute

Not Very Demure

As y'all would say

Chile, a hot mess!

So, I am hiding myself in the dark until I develop into the
person

That you are no longer use to

The person you weren't introduce to

I am in the fixer state

Until I can be exposed to light without damage

The Moments We Don't Speak Of

It's The moments we don't speak of ...hiding our fears.
Showing our happy side to the world who doesn't see us
hide our tears.
These are the moments we don't speak of.
Struggling to get out of bed, and although making it our
last day runs through our heads.
We push on.
Swallowing our pain
Silencing our thoughts with alcohol trying to maintain
Although the volume of our thoughts stays the same
These are the moments we don't speak of.
Because we're taught not to complain, that crying will
make nothing change
Going insane
Losing are inner battles, but still we fight.
Brightening up the rooms with our dimmed lights,
Because we are the chosen ones.
The misfits, the black sheep and the unseen
The ones the world need because, we have a story to
tell...
One that can change the world.

Mr. Perfect

Mr. Perfect!
Look at you wearing that arrogance!
Don't forget your entitlement
You look Sharp!
Manipulation at its finest!
Did you look into the mirror?
Was I in your reflection?
because you're pointing fingers at me
Are you giving me credit, for your inflated self-esteem?
Oh, you shouldn't have
I didn't know you had so many skeletons in your closet
Thats why you be judging, everybody else's
Cause' you got it going on!
So, were you going?
Do you have a place in mind
If I may offer a suggestion
Hell will do just fine.
They offer unlimited preferential treatment
And preferred seating for
for all of your attention seeking, needs.
So how are you getting there?
Never mind that, I know how you roll
You're going to drive because you like to be in control

But if you park at Self-center location
They Offer Validation
I know you'll like that right?
I'm excited for you because this, is, going to be, a
Grandiose night!
Don't forget your bad mood and anger issues in case you
get a little cold
Ok, one more look at you before I let you go
Yup you're such a narcissist!
Ok now hurry out before reality rips you apart
And remember whatever you do
it's never your fault!

Forgive Yourself

Give yourself grace
You did the best you could with what you had
You can't change the past
ok you did some bad
but who doesn't make mistakes
Failing is what it takes to grow
Let your self-hatred go
fall in love with you again
So what you fell
pick yourself up and begin again.
Hug your inner child
Tell them they are not to blame
for any of your pain
You are not your past so embrace your journey to change
Don't allow any person to decide your fate
It's not too late
Forgive yourself as you have forgiven others
Renew your mind
Don't let negativity get you down
Forget the what the nay sayers have to say
You're a better person now

A World with Just Me

Do you know what would be funny?
A world with just me in it
laughing at my own jokes may send me crazy
You would think I may get lonely
But just maybe, if there was a world with just me
I would be forced to Hug myself
I would have no choice but to spend time with myself
I would fall in love with the kinky coils in my hair,
I'll admire my own body
I would love me
I would invest in me
I would pick myself up
Pat myself on my back
Speak life into me
Give back to me
I would live by my own rules
 unapologetically
I would be forced to choose me

I am Trying

I'm trying to be the best that I can be
But lately it's like I can't be great
People testing me, while God is testing me
like daughter choose your fate
I've been trying to make my family proud
I'm having doubts that it's too late
They say to be successful, try going around a richer crowd
But I don't think I can relate
do they know what's on my plate?
I'm trying
Smiling on the outside but on the inside, I'm dying
I'm trying to pay these bills, but my cards are steadily declining
Please don't judge the way I choose to hustle I'm basically surviving
I've been standing tall, taking a leap of faith trying to come up with a plan
*One foot after another until depression comes than knock me on my a***
Ya'll I'm trying
Sometimes I want to be left alone, and I'll go silent for days
It's just that hunger for success will put you in some

introverted ways
But I'm trying y'all
I'm trying
People aren't what they pretend to be
Calling out the fakeness now I'm gaining way more
enemies
I'm trying y'all
I had a man do me wrong
My pride didn't like him clowning me
Broken hearts had me climbing up on balconies
Yeah, love is my weakness so I guess you can say pain
strengthened me
Love has taken wind from me
people stringing me along you would think that it's a
symphony
nobody offering sympathy
But I'm trying
I had a friend tell me choose light
and that got me through the night
I been trying to choose light but can't see to get it right
I've been trying to choose a new path and I'm not sure
what's way to go
And karmas been getting back at me
They say you reap whatever you sow.so I'm replenishing
my soul
I've been getting it out of the mud, But the mud has been
getting thicker

*I'm trying to pour into myself, but all of my cups have
been filled with liquor
Building fame but it's not making me richer
I've been trying y'all
Laughing to keep from crying
Bills piling on the table but that isn't none of y'all
problem
I've been trying to do right
Good friend told me come up out of the darkness don't
let them steal your light
Look forward to your future because that's beautiful
sight
But all of my life I had to fight
And I'm not stopping now
I have family faith and God, and I know he's going to
hold me down
I'm not rich, I'm not poor
Still struggling to survive but I'm not begging anymore
Everything I ever lost is going to get replaced
To many doors been shut in my face
I'm coming back with the keys
I'm not knocking anymore
I don't need a tour, guide, I've seen hell and back through
my owns eyes
Learned to survive with my mother in the kitchen
I've been through the trenches
Thank God for her I never slept on any benches she was*

trying y'all
But I've been keeping it together
hoping it'll get better
Praying through it all
Trying to keep my hands from going through people's
jaws
Yeah, I got a few but I'm working on it y'all
Laughing to keep from crying
Smiling on the outside but on the inside, I'm dying
But I'm trying y'all
I'm trying

Addiction is Mental

Every day feels the same
I drop the girls off at school,
then I am headed to my favorite coffee shop, right before
work
We all have our thing that either quiets the mind or
make them louder
Mine was coffee

It provided a sense of calmness
It put me in a mood, and I was hooked
but to the routine, not the coffee
We tend to hold on to things, we don't really need
until it's part of our daily routine
and we call it addiction

The mind plays tricks on you
we're conditioned to believe that our
addictions are must haves, and we can't put them down
when in all reality we're just use to having them around
and once we wake up without it
we panic, we fear, we get all shaken up
Because the thing that we're used to having close
is now out of touch
And to get it back, we'll go to the extreme

not knowing that the things we call addictions we don't
really need

48

The song's been over

I can feel it dying the more that we try
But our connection's lost like Wi-Fi
and we don't want to let it go
Because we both invested way too much
But still we're looking for a way out
Pulled up with high hopes but we
Spent the block with more doubts
We're stuck pretending for days
we found ourselves caught in a maze
once again looking for a way out
I admit we're stuck in our ways
Singing our favorite part of the song
Hitting the replay
using what used to be for a reason to stay
When the song's been over
It's not anyone's fault
people tend to drift a part
and there's a part of me that wants you to stay the
journey
But we need the time away, for self-reflecting
and healing, to grow
and then we may know,
if this is where our hearts truly belong

If I Could Replace Guns with Books

I still drive my kids to school
Because,
Beefs are not private
And bullets are open to the public
And bodies drop on those bus stops

If I could, I would replace Guns with Books
Because,
Maybe then they'll actually pick one up
Schools will no longer have to check back packs
Because
Maybe then they'll actually have books in them
When my two brown brothers end up beefing with one
another
I'd rather, he throws a book at him, then to shoot him
And when it's all over
I'd rather, it be knowledge exchanged then a bullet

If only, books had the same value that a gun has
Then maybe bookshelves would clear fast
The tittle wouldn't be, "another little black kid found
dead"
or "another Black kid shot in the head"

Instead,
I'll be "another black kid, with Degrees and Honorees"

If Forensics get a hold of a book
The only connections they'll have to the streets would be
to teach
and not connections linked
To a teens murderer
The next time the police pulls and black person over
They'll actually respect the 1st and 4th amendments
and literally read them their rights and do what's right
and the black man won't fear for his life
and confidently exercise his rights
with a book drawn at him

26. Don't suffer in silence

We live in a world where mental instability is an
embarrassment and that seeking professional help
will stick with you and follow you for the rest of your
life, causing havoc, damaging your reputation
We fear that as soon as we get help, there goes our job,
there goes that license to carry, and maybe it'll
even be used against us in a custody battle. we fear that
admitting to needing a little mental support may make
us less desirable. We believe that we may lose
friendships and big opportunities, so we suffer in silence.
I challenge you to be brave, to speak up, to speak freely
and get help. You are not alone!
I need you to survive, because you matter! I promise. It
doesn't matter if you are homeless, addicted to drugs, in
prison
a single mother, a single father, your girlfriend left,
boyfriend left, going through a divorce, you may be
sleeping in your car, struggling to provide for your
family, you've got evicted, or maybe you just feel like
you're a burden. There is someone you matter too.
Maybe it's the stranger you smiled at. Maybe it's the
person you allowed to cut the line in front of you. Even
when life gets you down, look up and around. Live to tell

your story, so you can help someone else tell theirs. Do not suffer in silence.